Copyright Elaine R Snyder and WriteFreely 2019

All rights reserved

This is a work of fiction, and any resemblance to real people or events, real or imagined, is accidental.

Art created by Elaine R Snyder is representative of the poetic expression incorporated into this published work, not of the original media from which it was utilized. Under copyright, all images were created using print media which has been artistically altered within the confines of lawful use. All original images have been altered beyond the original by removing elements of the original and combining these elements with other print material to create an entirely new image as collage. None of the images used are representative of the original intent for which they were created, as they have been altered for artistic expression.

# The Story of Anyone Who Has Never Been Seen, Never Been Heard

Elaine R Snyder

*To the oppressed of the world, this work of art is for you. May it bring you hope, and help you to see you have brothers and sisters waiting for you in the light. You are worthy of love, justice, kindness, compassion, assistance, safety, friendship, and equality. Those you have been seeking are looking for you, too. Believe, and you will find them.*

*Dear Oppressors,*

I finally see liberty, a once-clouded star.

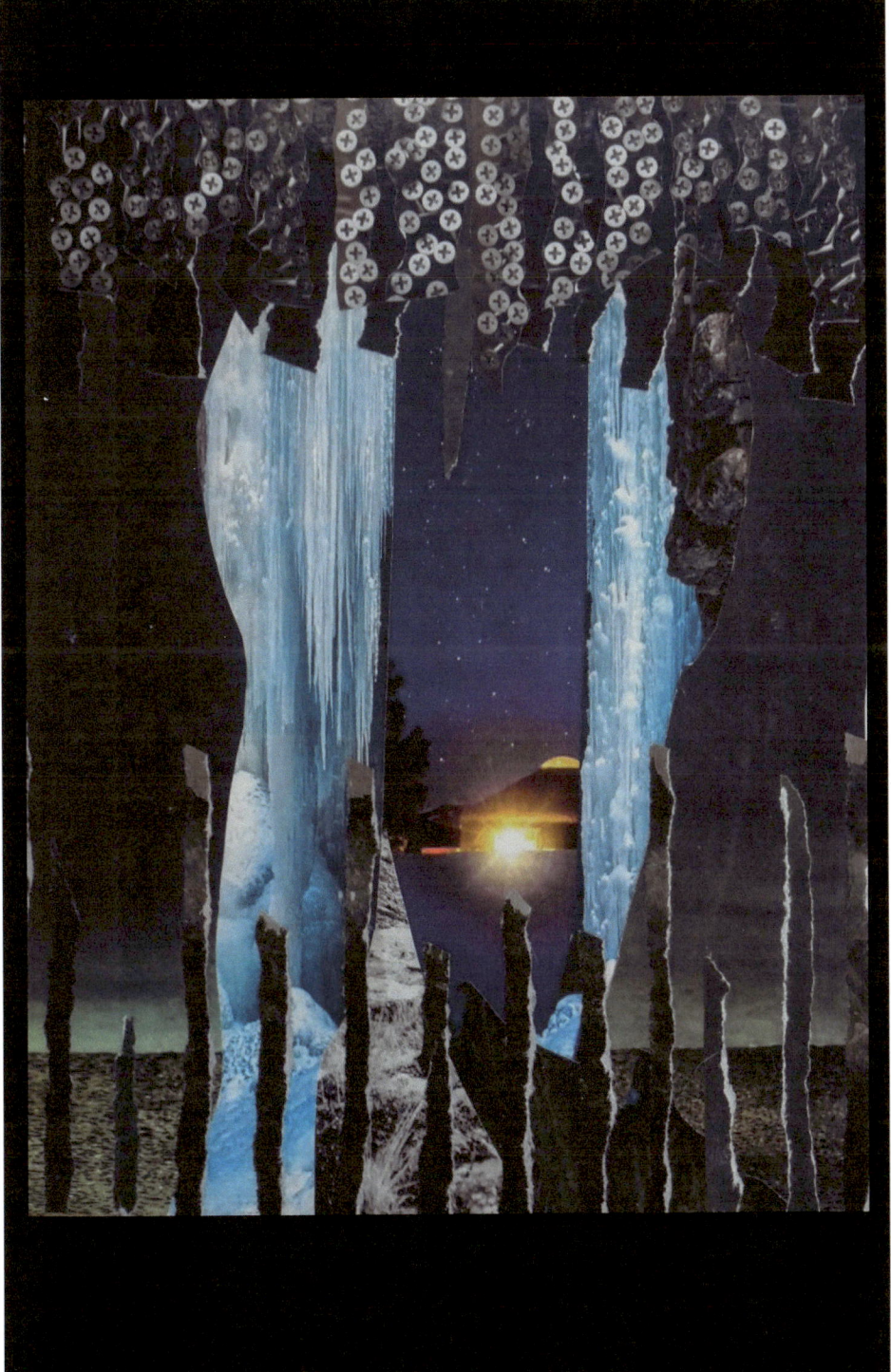

My body wishes to crowd around the light,
A sheltering cove, a hopeful suggestion
Flung outward in a room of acquaintances.

You had me wilted
Into the secret darkness you called freedom.
I walked over those unlit shores,
Believing the water as shallow as you said.

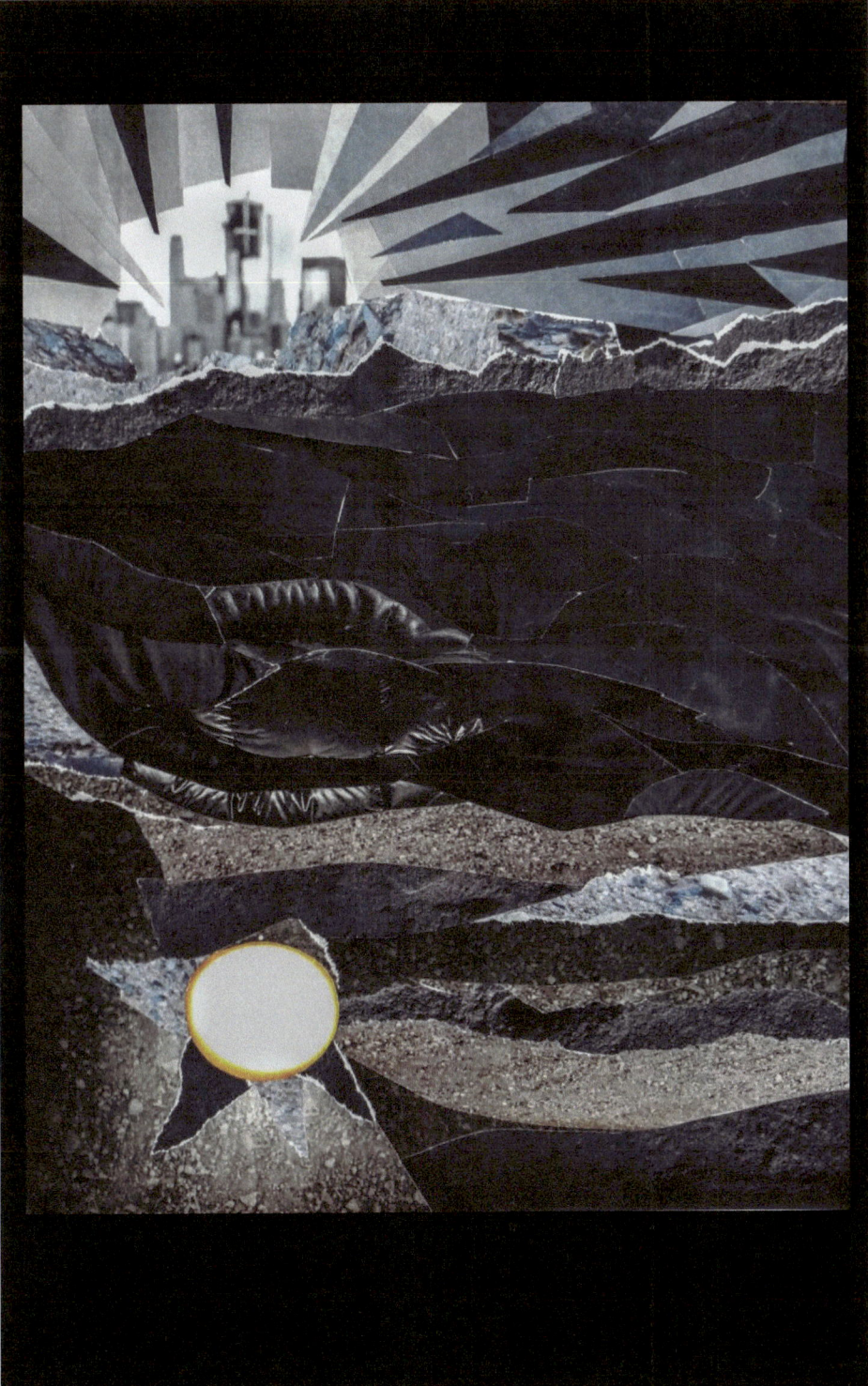

In the lack of light, the truth
Washed against my shod feet at regular,
Timely, and faithful intervals.
In my pockets I carried heavy stories,
Clinking against each other,
Noise which filled the time.

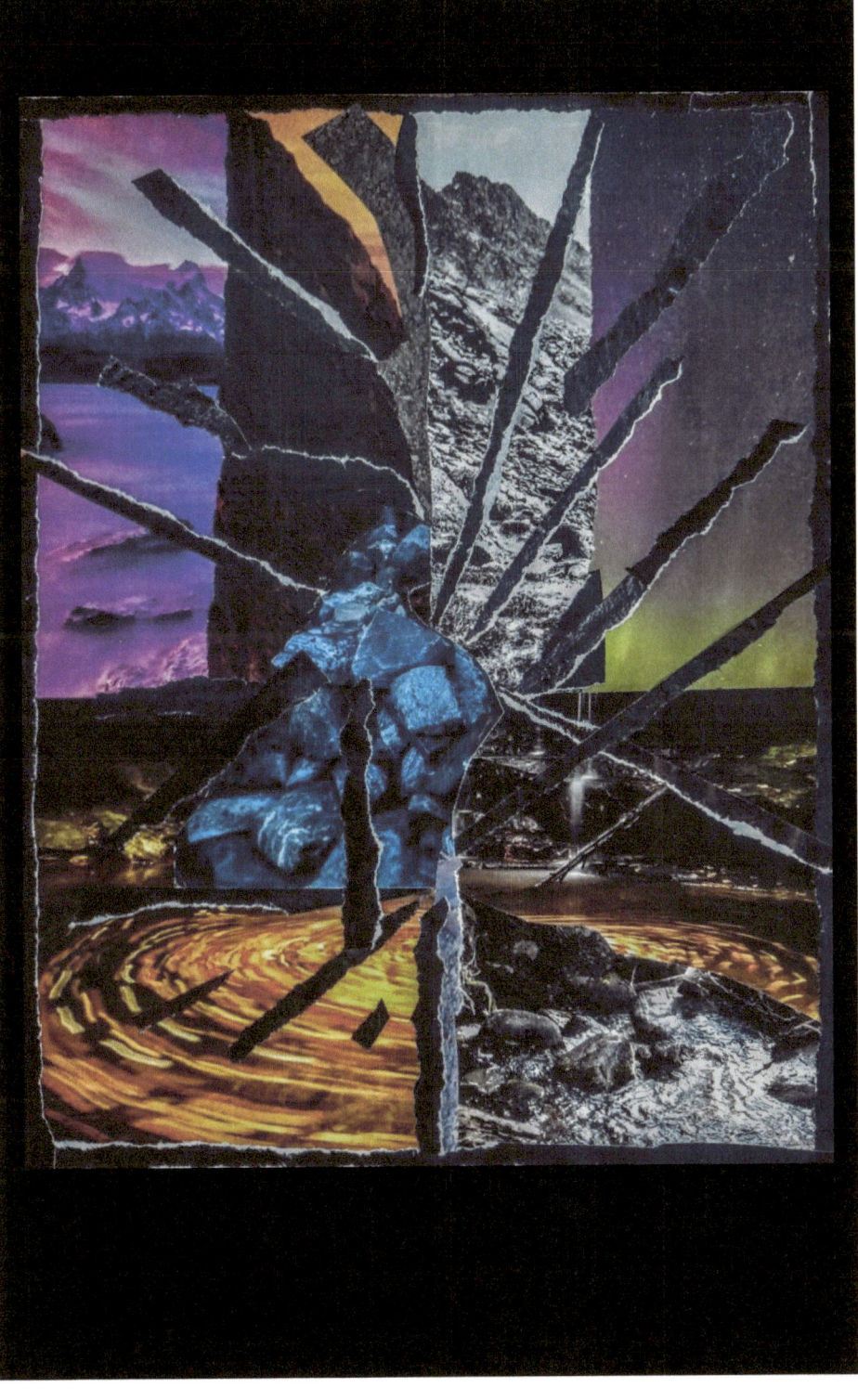

A break in the endless waves pulled back
The veil of darkness to which I was so accustomed.
Turning my head for the silence, in awe,
Seeing the shore littered with bodies for the
First time paralyzed me with despair.

When I could stand again,
I walked for a while in mourning, astonishment.
I wept at the death, the arms outstretched for help,
The rictus of their last moments still trapped
On their faces, the words they wanted to say
Forever clasped to the hollows of their mouths.
The heavy stories in my pocket echoed against
Walls I did not know were there.

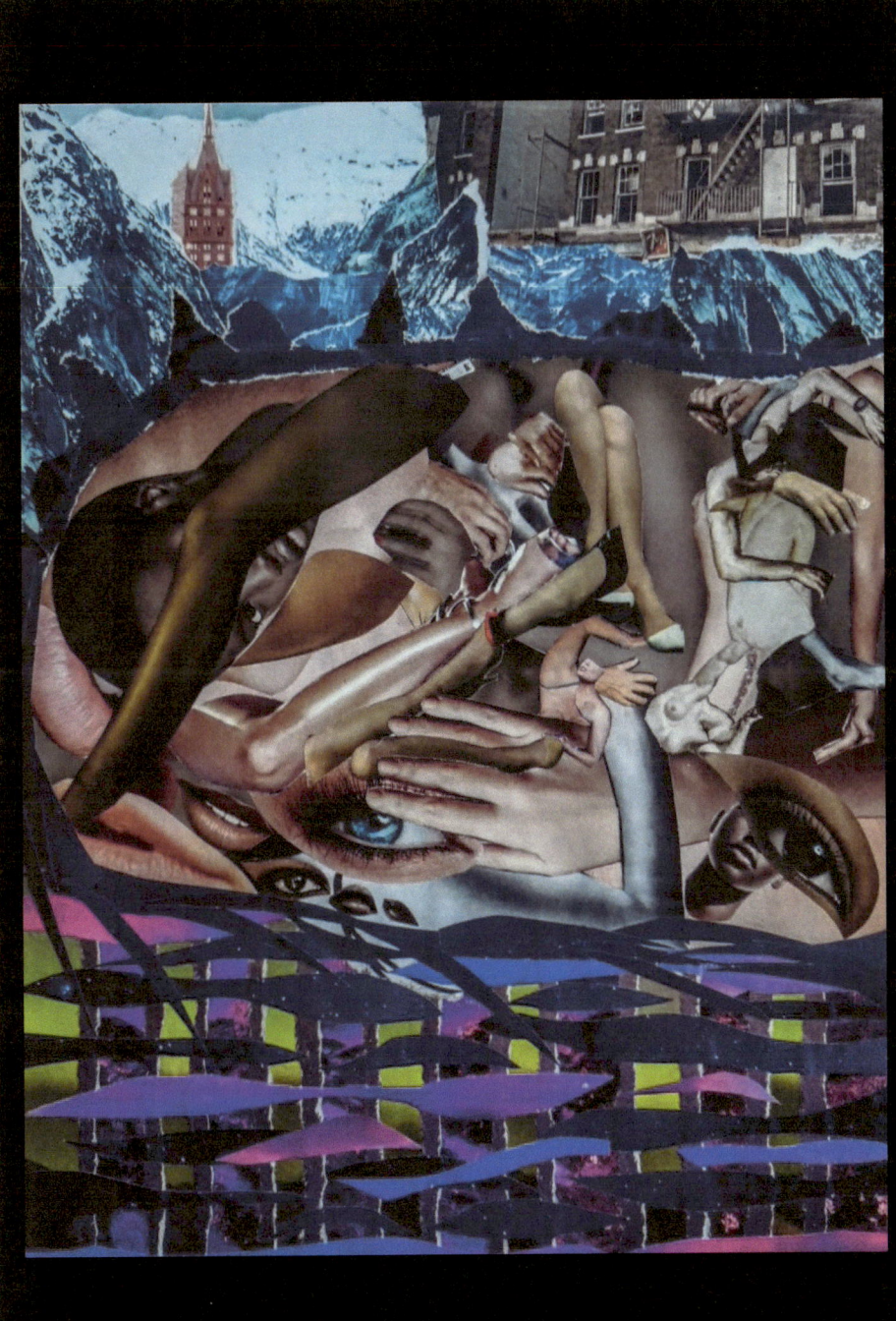

In the brightening light, no longer shuffling by feel,
The bodies, collapsed in their infinite variety,
All told the same story. Mine told that story, too.

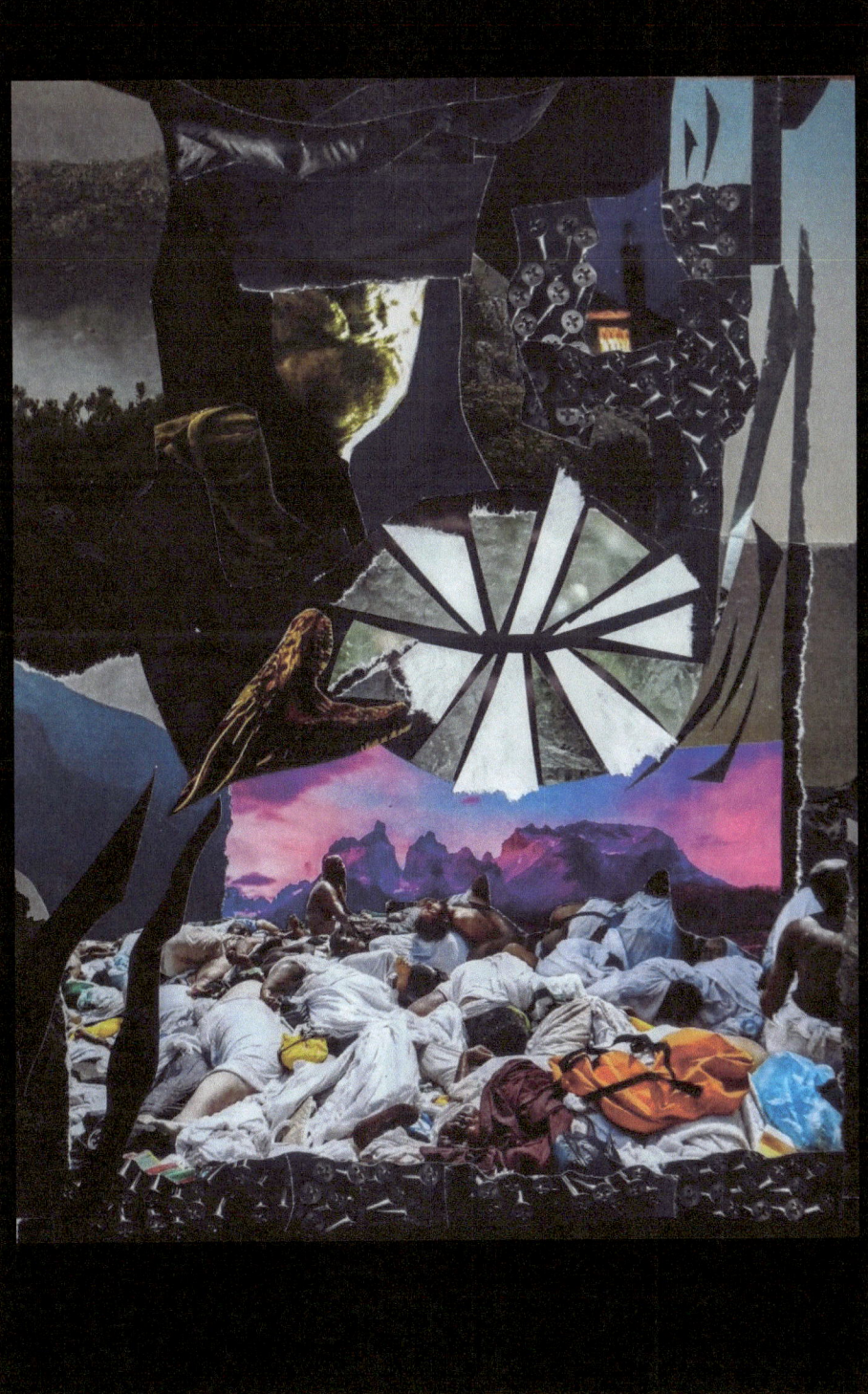

In the secret darkness, stories fall easily
From one hand to another. We accept them without
Knowing how shallow the plot, how collectively
Inane the characters, how obviously vile its villains.
How could we know?

We were forced to feel them out with our hands,
Reaching into dark spaces without knowing
What may happen, and because terrors came
To steal us, to maim us, to break us into parts,
Many of us did not dare to reach outward at all.
Fear silences many motivations.

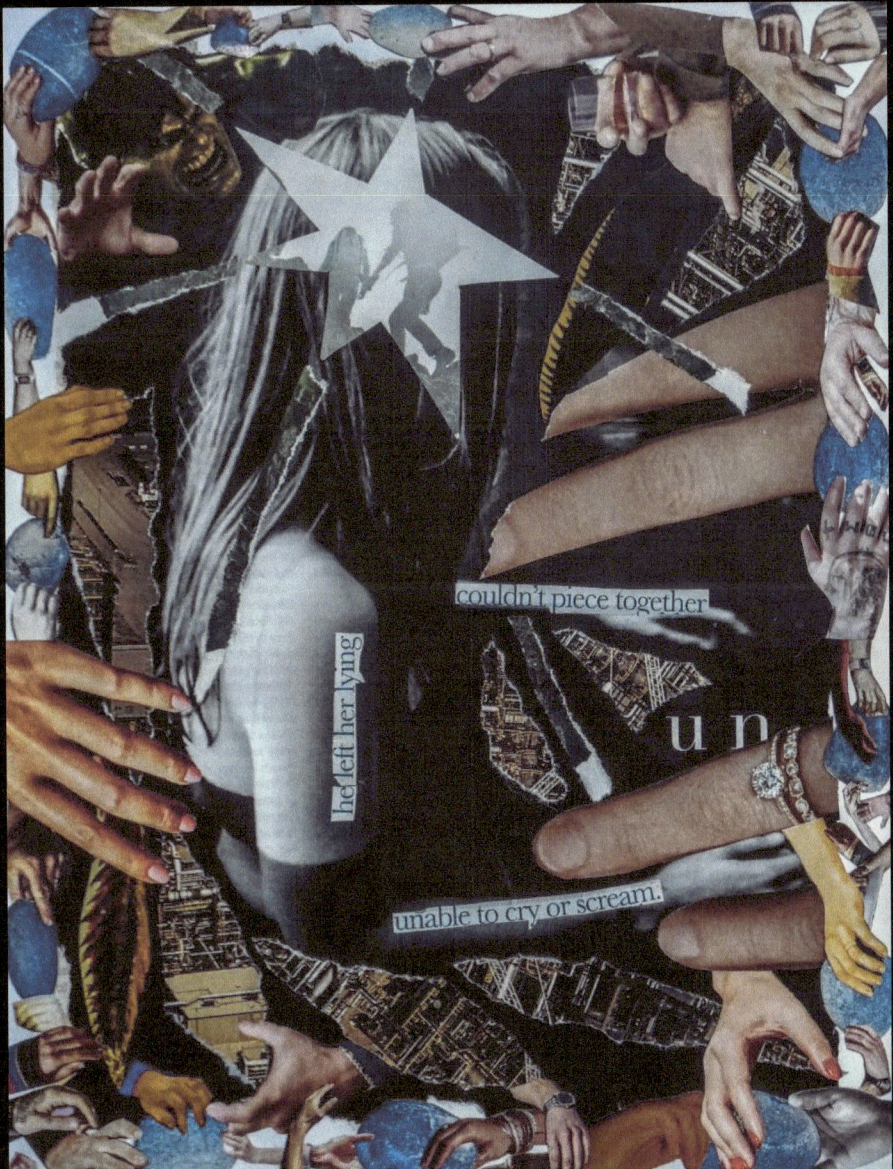

Still, throwing our hands out could offer
Rewards, small truths which fortune
Might unite like a puzzle.
Some of us put together the parts,
Washed against our heels, bumping in the tide,
And began to glimpse the larger framework.

We built a sketchy outline,
Better described as a poorly-constructed
Shanty town which leaned at the desperate
Edge of a gleaming city encapsulated by walls
Too high to climb.

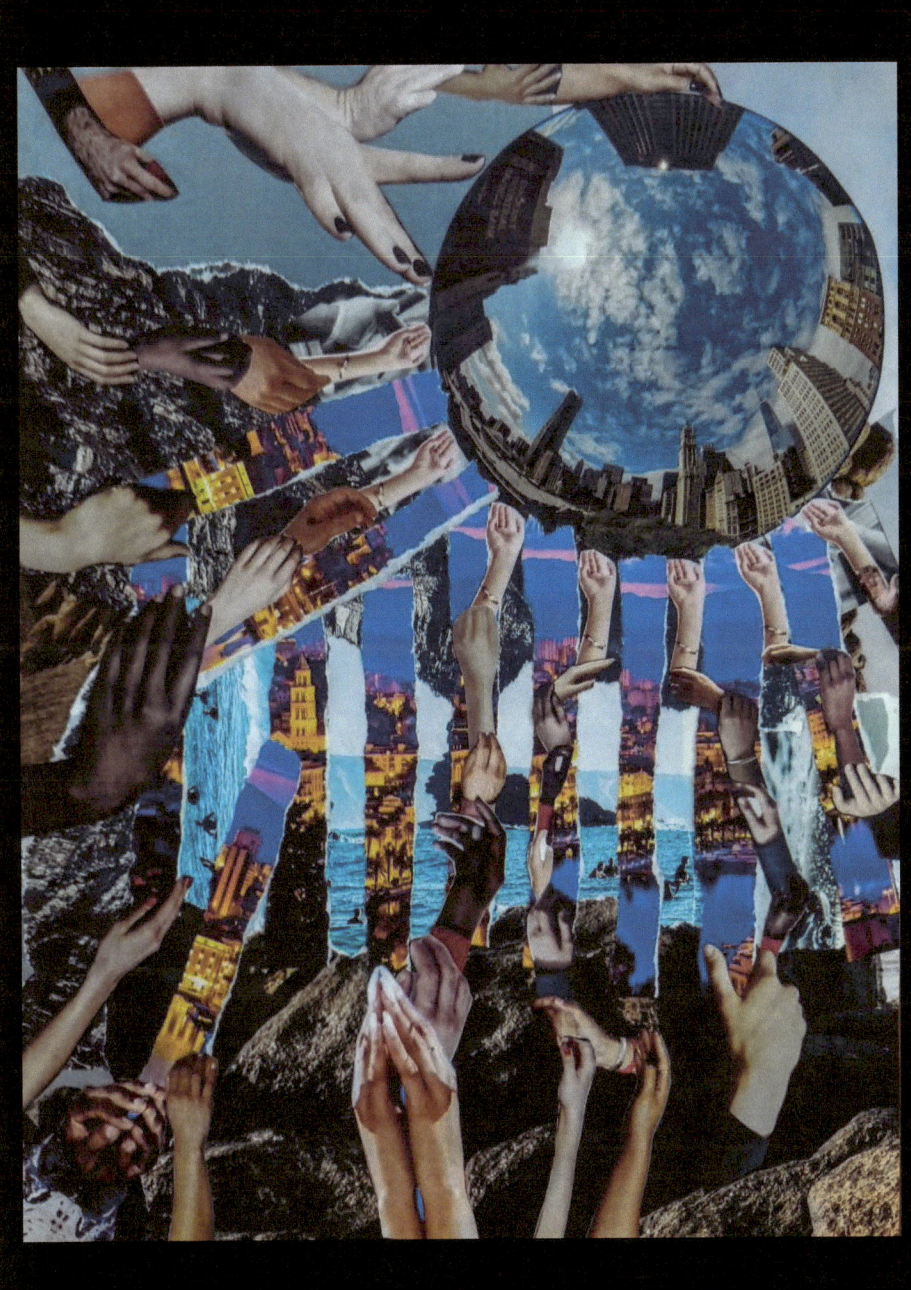

We gaze upon the unending horizon of oppression
And we know even more sorrow than the secret
Darkness of the lies through which we stumbled

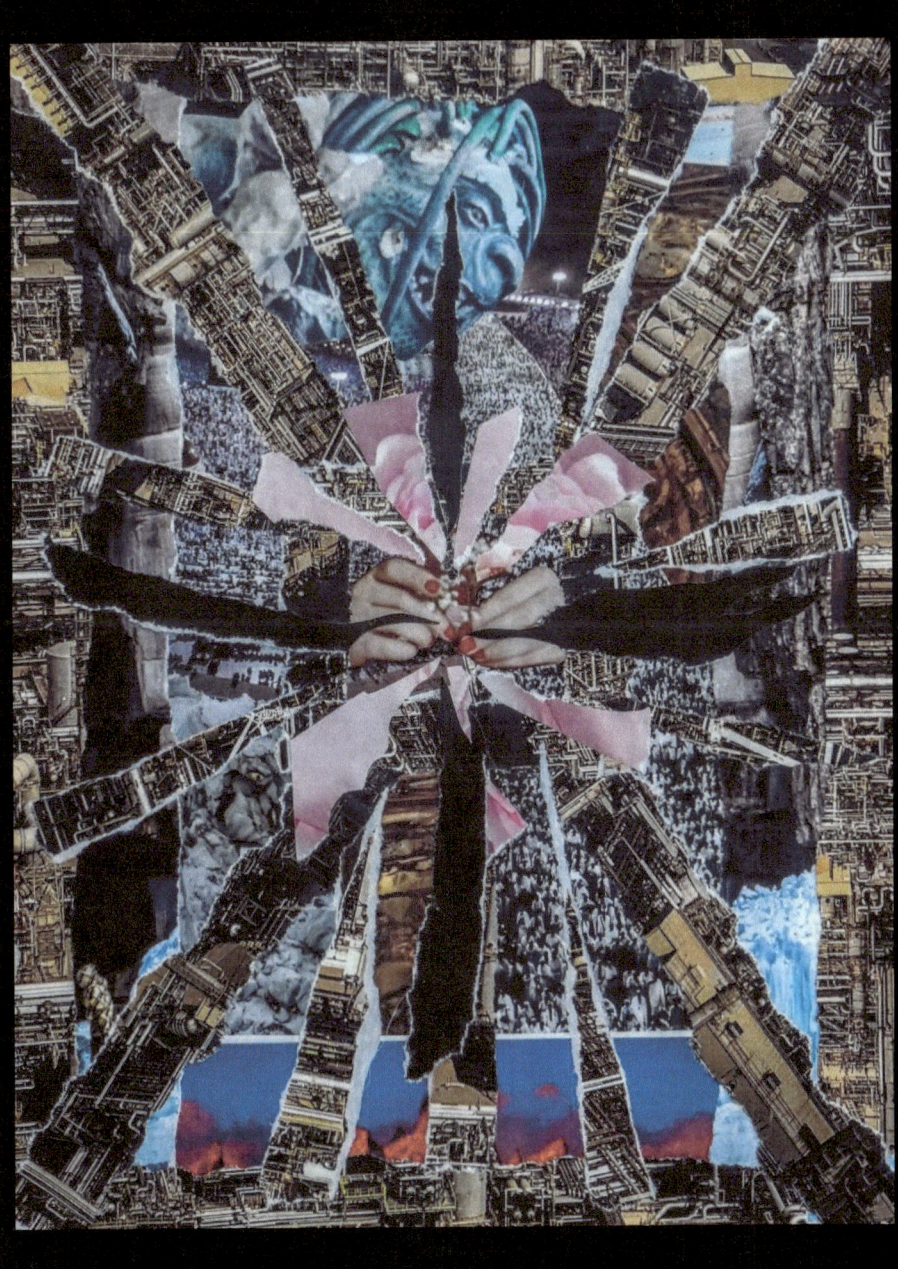

Eventually we become accustomed to seeing
The bodies which resolve into mere debris,
Which we must leave aside in order to keep shuffling
Forward until we find others like us, others
Who no longer crumple downward in small circles, others
Who also have discovered the light of
Liberty and curve, dome-like around their hungry stars

We collect ourselves into groups where we cling
To the raft of bodies.
In waves we rise,
Holding up the bodies in pyramids,
Handing down stones of stories, the truth we have
Built with our fingers in darkness, the rickety
Structure of dreams and whispers and nightmares
And half-healed sutures.

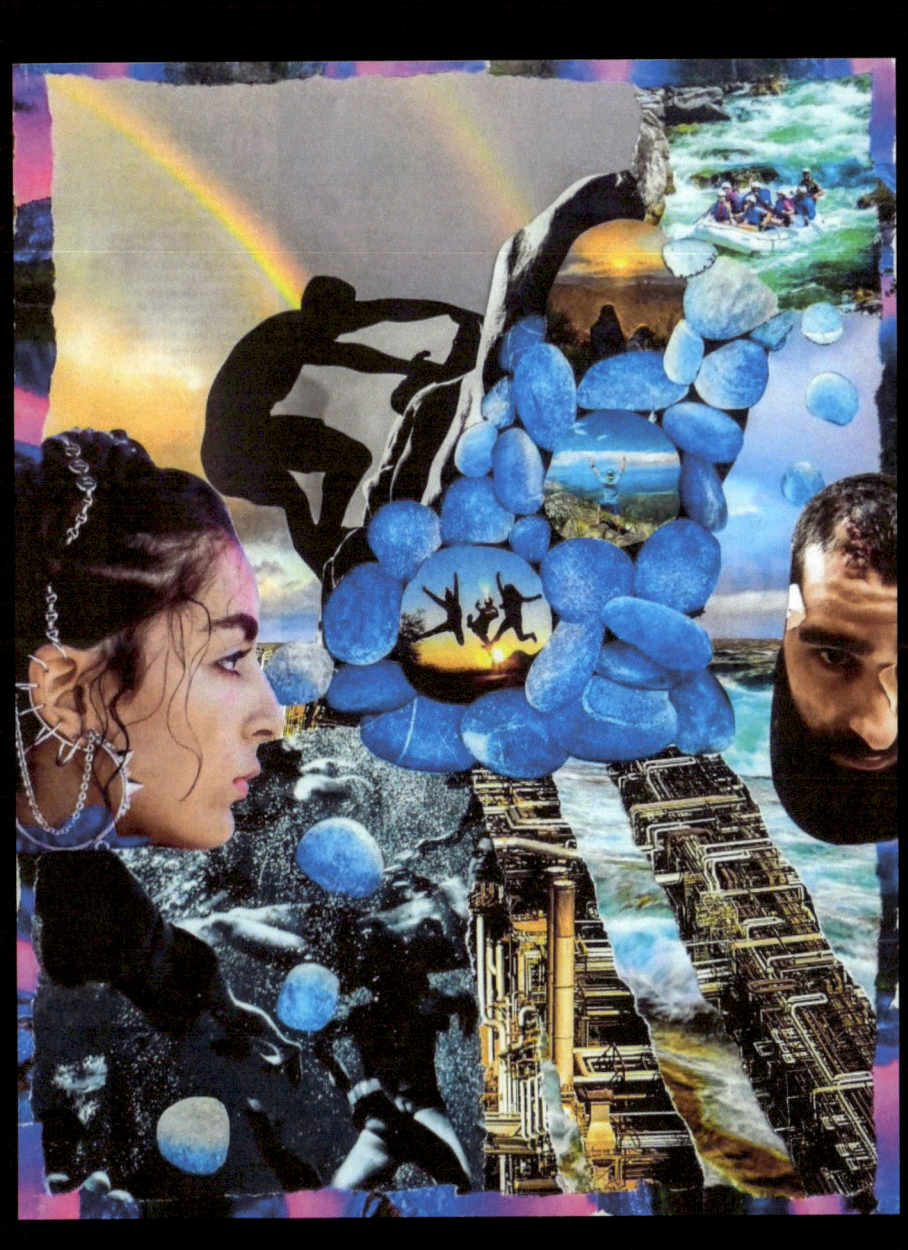

None of us knows all the truth. All of us know the
Whole story. We share in snatched moments,
Carefully riveted, clumsily erected,
In our universities of suffering; we gather the
Promises of scholarship, of our collected secrets,

And soon we begin to teach each other how to
Break the structure of what we survived,
Tearing away old clothes and cheap trinkets, tossing
Them atop the bonfire we build higher
And wider along the shores, drawing
More and more of us to the beacon,
Hands reaching out no longer in fumbling supplication,
But with purposeful resignation.

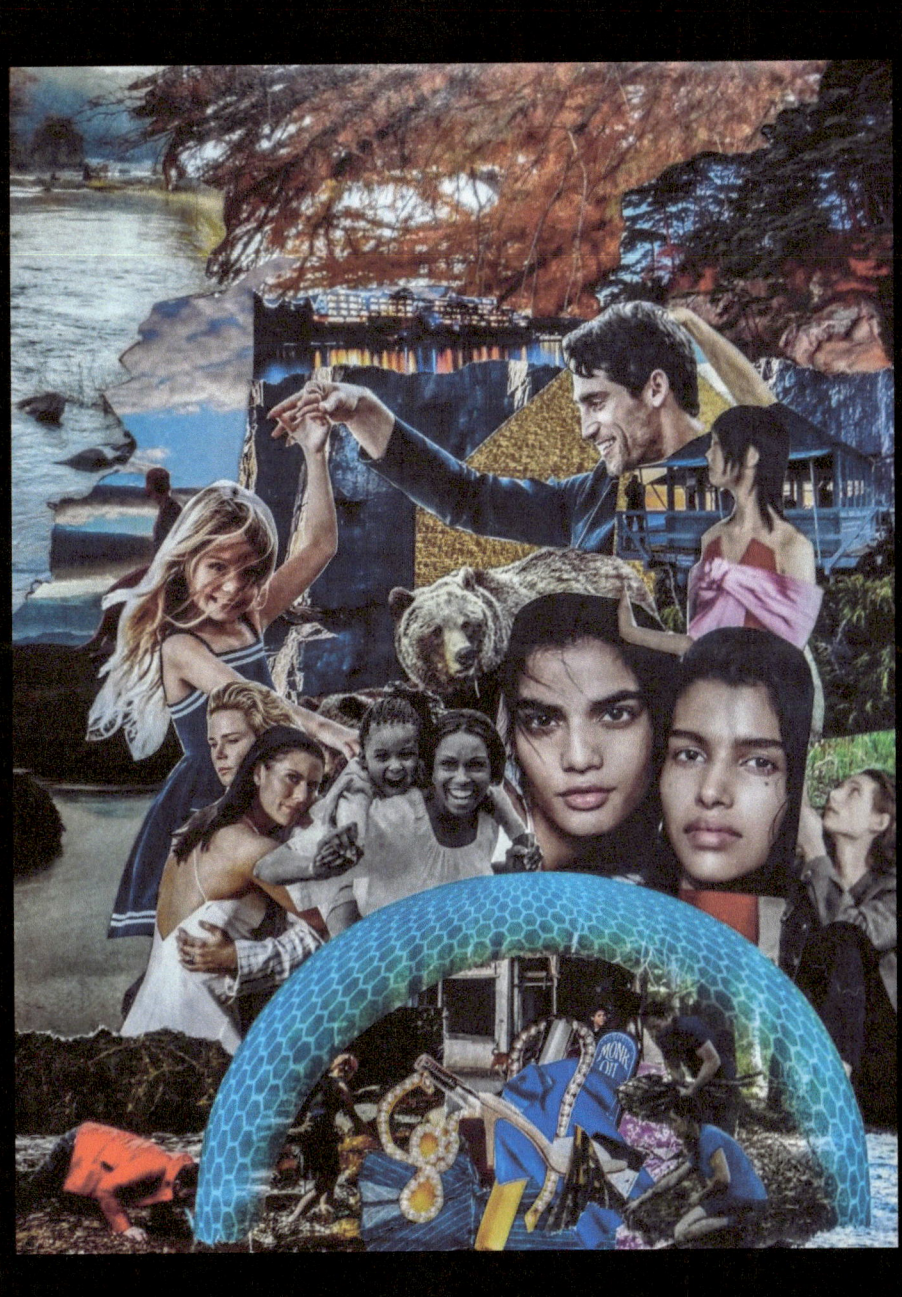

We build pyramids of fuel,
Pyramids of stories, pyramids of graves,
Pyramids of love and compassion.
We build with shared purpose.

The fire of liberty is burning.
We are naked in its embers.
It lights up the walls of your gleaming cities.
It exposes the bodies of your victims.
It colors the darkness with gold.

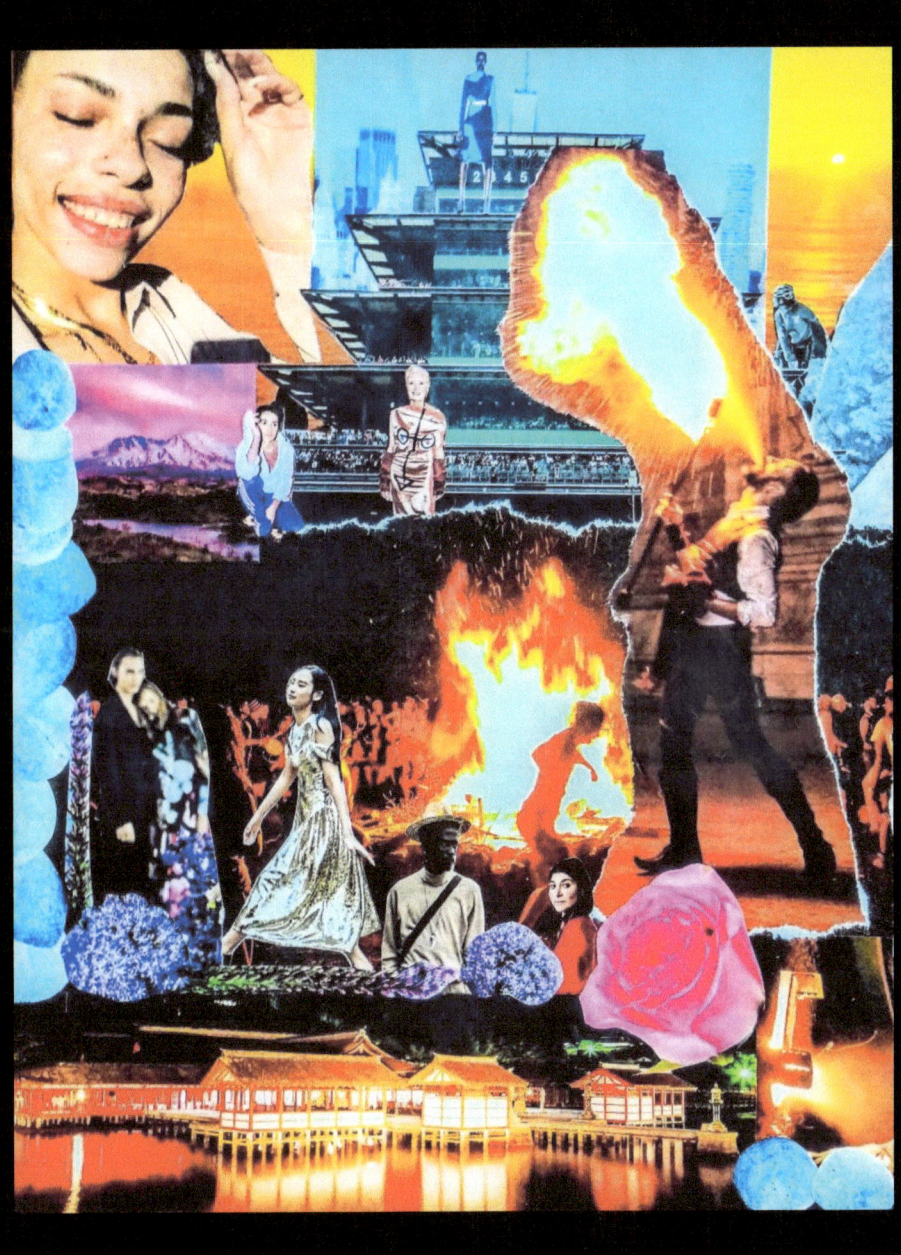

Signed,
The Oppressed

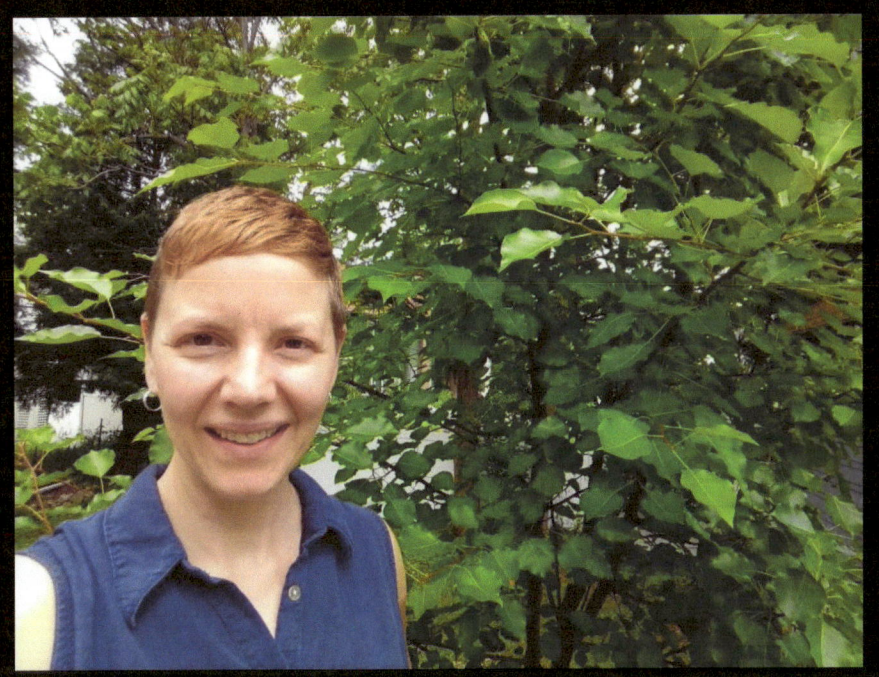

Elaine R Snyder is the author of five books, and is also a speaker and instructor of writing for empowerment and personal growth. She is available to teach workshops and offer lectures on empowerment, especially for survivors. You can find her books, contact her for events, and read her blog, *Logophile*, at [elainersnyder.com](elainersnyder.com).

www.ingramcontent.com/pod-product-compliance
Lightning Source LLC
Chambersburg PA
CBHW040303220526
45473CB00002B/567